Vegan Cookbook For Female Athletes

A Beginner's Guide to Veganism and Curated Collection of 20 Plant-Based Recipes To Increase Performance

Copyright © 2020 Larry Jamesonn
All rights reserved. No portion of this book may be reproduced in any form without permission from the publisher, except as permitted by U.S. copyright law.

Disclaimer

By reading this disclaimer, you are accepting the terms of the disclaimer in full. If you disagree with this disclaimer, please do not read the book. The content in this book is provided for informational and educational purposes only.

This book is not intended to be a substitute for the original work of this diet plan. At most, this book is intended to be a beginner's supplement to the original work for this diet plan and never acts as a direct substitute. This book is an overview, review, and commentary on the facts of that diet plan.

All product names, diet plans, or names used in this book are for identification purposes only and are property of their respective owners. The use of these names does not imply endorsement. All other trademarks cited herein are the property of their respective owners.

None of the information in this book should be accepted as an independent medical or other professional advice.

The information in the books has been compiled from various sources that are deemed reliable. It has been analyzed and summarized to the best of the Author's ability, knowledge, and belief. However, the Author cannot guarantee the accuracy and thus should not be held liable for any errors.

You acknowledge and agree that the Author of this book will not be held liable for any damages, costs, expenses, resulting from the application of the information in this book, whether directly or indirectly. You acknowledge and agree that you assume all risk and responsibility for any action you undertake in response to the information in this book.

You acknowledge and agree that by continuing to read this book, you will (where applicable, appropriate, or necessary) consult a qualified medical professional on this information. The information in this book is not intended to be any sort of medical advice and should not be used in lieu of any medical advice by a licensed and qualified medical professional.

Always seek the advice of your physician or another qualified health provider with any issues or questions you might have regarding any sort of medical condition. Do not ever disregard any qualified professional medical advice or delay seeking that advice because of anything you have read in this book.

Table of Contents

Chapter 1: Introduction 7
Chapter 2: The Beginner Vegan 10
Chapter 3: Vegan Foods 14
Chapter 4: Veganism for Female Athletes 16
Chapter 5: Vegan Recipes 24
Chapter 6: Bonus Recipes 28

Chapter 1: Introduction

Did you know that the United States is one of the leading countries spearheading the vegan movement? As of 2019, approximately 4% of the adult American population does not consume any form of meat.

A certain percentage of this population are female athletes, both professional and amateur athletes who choose to abstain from animal products as well.

We are seeing more of this trend progressing as time goes on and it's visible any time you go to a grocery store. Just take a walk down the dairy aisle and you will see plant-based butter, and non dairy milk substitutes.

This guide is meant to provide female athletes with an overview of veganism and how it pertains specifically for them. The guide first provides a brief overview of veganism and then discusses specifics on how female athletes can adopt this type of eating philosophy into their day to day plan. Lastly, the guide provides a curated collection of vegan recipes to help inspire you in your journey towards veganism.

In this guide you will discover:
- What veganism is and how it's different from vegetarianism
- Positive reasons to adopt veganism

- How to jumpstart your vegan journey (for a beginner)
- 2 crucial minerals needed by female atheletes
- Examples of female athletes who adopted veganism
- A "cheatsheet" of practical tips on how to get more of the 2 crucial minerals into your body
- A curated collection of delicious vegan recipes

What is Veganism?
Veganism is a way of life for some people, it is dietary choice or style of living where people refrain completely from all animal based products including meat, fish, duck, turkey, eggs, cheese, milk, butter, seafood, cream, honey, and every other product from animal origin. This is different from vegetarianism, which may permit certain animal products.

Some people who embrace veganism also go beyond dietary borders and will ensure that their entire way of life is in tranquility with treating animals with kindness and respect, such as abstaining from purchasing leather or fur garments and bags, and not purchasing any products such as make-up, kitchenware or furniture where animals have been used to make or test these products in any way.

What Are Some Reasons to Adopt Veganism?

To avoid animal based food-borne disease

For animal rights: many people adopt this lifestyle for animal rights, due to the ways animals are cruelly slaughtered, caged, fed, injected and treated for meat or dairy.

For the environment: many people abstain from animal-based products to help save the environment.

Vegan food tastes great: A person who adopts veganism will eat a diet high in natural foods including fresh fruits and vegetables, nuts and seeds, berries and dried fruit, sprouts and herbs, fresh juices and smoothies, wholegrains, legumes and beans, chocolate and dairy-free treats such as cakes, muffins and slices.

For health benefits: This includes weight loss, healthy skin elimination of allergies, increases longevity, increases energy, strengthens nails, healthier hair, reduces saturated fats, prevents heart attack and stroke, treats or reverses some cancers, alleviates arthritis.

To save money: meat and dairy are expensive.

Chapter 2: The Beginner Vegan

Making the shift to a vegan diet for the first time can be intimidating yet exciting at the same time. Below is a list of 10 helpful tips for those who are new to the vegan diet, focusing on how to smoothly start a vegan diet and how to ensure that the transition to becoming vegan is as easy and stress-free as possible.

1. Research and Gather Information: Before you make any kind of lifestyle change, it is always a good idea to do plenty of research beforehand. By doing so, you will know exactly what to expect. You need to gather information on what vegans do and don't eat, what benefits, what obstacles and challenges vegans face, etc. You will thank yourself later on for your thorough research.

2. What Do You Want To Achieve? For the beginner vegan, always write down on paper exactly what you want to achieve on the vegan lifestyle. Although you might want to perform better as a female athlete through veganism, you might certainly have other reasons for turning vegan as well. Be it weight loss, to clear up skin conditions e.g.: acne, psoriasis, eczema, to achieve inner peace, to reduce allergies, to reverse chronic illness, to concentrate better, to help save the

planet, animal rights, etc. Whatever your reasons are for making the transition to the vegan diet, write them down on paper. Stick them where you can see them every day such as on the fridge.

3. Find Good Recipes: It is absolutely necessary to find and collect some good vegan recipes, since you will be doing a lot of different cooking from now on. You need to find some quick and easy recipes for the times when you are too tired or busy to cook anything fancy. Also gather a wide assortment of vegan recipes including vegan breakfast recipes, lunches, dinners, snacks, cakes, slices, desserts, etc... Find your recipes online, purchase a vegan recipe e-book and make sure you have your vegan recipe folder well-prepared before starting your new vegan lifestyle.

4. Let Family and Friends Know: Let your beloved ones know as soon as you make the decision to become vegan. This will ensure that when you visit them, or when they visit you, food will not be a problem since they have already been informed about your new vegan diet.

5. Be Prepared For Cravings: When you stop eating certain foods, you will inevitably have food cravings from time to time. Be prepared for this and make

sure you have some healthy snacks or frozen baking easily accessible so you don't cave in. Find some recipes also for "vegan clones" of your favorite meals and snacks (Note: Professional vegan chefs have written an assortment of recipe e-books to cater for your cravings).

6. **Know Your Vegan Food Brands:** Nowadays the supermarkets and health shops tailor to the needs of the vegan, so you should have no trouble finding meat-free, dairy-free snacks and foods such as vegan cheese, tofu, vegan chocolate, health bars, "bacon" and cereal. Try them all out and get to know your favorites.

7. **Stay Motivated Online:** There are many vegan online support groups, chat rooms and blogs that you can visit and interact with fellow vegans online. This will help you to stay motivated, encouraged, and will also help you to realize that you are not the only vegan on the planet.

8. **Enjoy Your Fruit and Vegetable Shopping:** You will be eating more fresh produce now that you are vegan. Find some fruit and vegetable markets or food stores that deliver quality produce at a reasonable price. Keep in mind that supermarkets are often more expensive. Enjoy choosing your fresh produce and

make your fruit and vegetable shopping a relaxing experience.

9. Bake Your Own Healthy Treats and Snacks: Since you will be limited to buying treats and sweets out at cafes and restaurants, bake your own vegan treats such as brownies, cakes, slices and muffins. Bake an entire batch every week and freeze in individual portions for when you need a treat.

10. Don't Give Up Easily: The transition to the vegan lifestyle is often the most difficult right at the beginning. After a while, it will become easier and easier until it becomes second-nature for you. So for the beginner vegan or those relatively new to the vegan lifestyle, my advice is not to give up straight away but to give your new lifestyle a fair chance. Chances are that after a few months you will be extremely grateful that you never gave up.

The rewards and benefits of this lifestyle always outweigh any challenges that you may face from time to time!

Chapter 3: Vegan Foods

What Do Vegans Eat?

Vegans primarily eat the following foods, but this may vary from individual to individual: vegetables, fresh fruits, whole-grains, pasta, olive oil, coconut oil, tofu, legumes and beans, soy, faux meats, faux cheese, legume patties, vegetable patties, dried fruit, soy and rice milk, soy yogurt, cakes, muffins, slices, brownies, salads, fresh juices, smoothies, nuts, seeds, peanut butter, almond butter, cashew butter, vegan margarine, vegetable soups, and stir-fries.

Vegan Meals at Restaurants

Some people do not like to cook every meal, or they are simply too busy. Most restaurants and take-away cafes offer vegan food and meals, including Italian tomato sauce pastas, vegetable minestrone etc., Chinese rice, vegetable spring rolls, vegetable stir-fry's, steamed vegetables, vegetable soups, tofu dishes, Indian rice, dahl, vegetable coconut milk curries, lentil dishes, Thai rice, vegetable curries, tofu noodle soups, coconut milk pumpkin soups etc., Subway, Sumo-Salad, etc. Infact, there's guarantee that you could find some vegan food options at nearly any restaurant, café or take-away shop nowadays! All you have to do is ask!

Vegan Food at the Supermarket

Since more and more people are becoming vegetarian and vegan every year, supermarkets and health stores are doing their part to keep up with the consumer's needs. This is excellent for the modern busy vegan, who often does not have the time or energy to cook every meal. The number of vegan products and brands are increasing every year, with more and more vegan food products "vegan fast food" surfacing on the shelves. This vegan fast food includes chocolate bars, muesli bars, packet chips, cereals, cookies, muffins, cakes, etc. Modern day vegan can absolutely fulfill their junk food desires with the opportunity of products available.

Chapter 4: Veganism for Female Athletes

Can Vegans Be Successful in Sports?

There is a common belief that to succeed in a sport, you need to eat meat and drink milk. It is thought by many that vegans won't have the necessary strength or stamina to beat meat eaters. These beliefs are false and based on a lack of knowledge.

There are some very successful vegans in the world. To become the best in any sport you need the dedication and focus to reach the top when there are so many distractions that could stop you. Not many people have that dedication. You need the right genes to give you the edge over your competitors. Very few have the right genes to make them champions.

There are two vegan strength champions that come to mind, though. Both women. Pat Reeves, is a world class British powerlifter. Another example is Jane Black, an olympic weight lifter who has set records in masters' lifting events.

What about men? Perhaps too many male strength athletes are worried about not getting enough of their usual slaughterhouse products. Again, give it some time for the truth to reach them. There are many vegans in training, as can be seen in the vegan fitness and bodybuilding forums.

Women's Nutrition Requirements in Sports

Female and male athletes respond to training in a fairly comparable way. As volume and intensity of training increases, so does aerobic capacity and hence performance. Body composition tends to change, whether male or female, indicating that physiologically, we are all actually quite similar.

Nutritionally speaking, the amount is similar between men and women. Regardless of the sport in question, energy intake must match energy output in order to fuel training and recovery. For endurance athletes, carbohydrate intake needs to be at approximately 7-10g per kg/bwt or 4g per lb/bwt. If this requirement is not met, performance tends to suffer, and fatigue creeps in.

It is important for any athlete, regardless of gender, to train and compete with optimum fuel reserves, and of course be well hydrated.

Iron and Calcium Requirements of the Female Athlete

Iron and calcium are crucial minerals needed by female athletes.

Iron

Levels of iron in the body are particularly important given iron's role in many enzyme functions and it's fundamental role in the formation of hemoglobin (75% of total body iron is in this form) and as a constituent of myoglobin (the O_2 carrying material that functions inside the cells).

Iron performs the overwhelming activity of transporting oxygen from the lungs to the mitochondria within muscle cells – this is a vital component for athletes.

Females have a higher rate of iron loss than that of men mainly via blood loss through menstruation, as well as during pregnancy and childbirth. This means that women generally need more iron than men.

An athlete's iron status measured by levels of blood haemoglobin, haematocrit concentration and plasma ferritin levels may further be compromised due to a number of factors directly related to training.

These have been identified as bleeding within the digestive system, inadequate diet and poor iron absorption, loss of iron through heavy sweating, red blood cell breakdown due to trauma created by certain high-impact activities (e.g. long-distance running), and even over-frequent blood donation.

Calcium

National surveys have consistently show that there are low calcium level in young and adult females as well as female athletes. This is normally due to low energy intake, fad diets, or poorly planned vegetarian and vegan diets. Inadequate calcium intake and consequently, poor calcium levels is compounded by diets that contain high phosphorous, high salt, high caffeine foods and drinks. These have a negative impact on calcium balance due to an increase in urinary calcium excretion.

Calcium and bone health: About 60% of adult bone is laid down during adolescence, when calcium deposition is at it's highest. This is due to increases in the hormones oestrogen, growth hormone and calcitriol. Mechanisms are put to work that lead to an overall stimulation of bone cell production and maturation. Bone resorption is out-weighed by bone deposition, leading to an increase in overall bone mineralisation. There seems to be a critical 4-year period during teenage years, from the ages of about 11-15 years, during which time most of the total gain in bone mineral density (BMD) and content (BMC) is accumulated.

Peak bone mass is a major determinant of osteoporosis in later life, so building the largest bone mass possible is one of the most important strategies to protect against osteoporosis in later life.

Females in the UK, aged 19-50 years, are thought to need at least 700mg calcium daily in order to meet the demands for calcium deposition in bone. Recommendations are lower than in most other industrialised countries and it has been suggested that 11-18 year olds require 1200-1500 mg/day to optimise peak bone mass.

Numerous well-controlled longitudinal studies have produced consistent positive effects of calcium supplementation on BMD in adolescent females, suggesting that UK reference values are sub-optimal.

Female athletes are a different sub-class all together with regard to calcium needs. Up to 400mg of calcium has been shown to be lost (in males) via sweat alone, from a 2-hr training session, and although calcium losses in females are unlikely to be that high, any female athlete such as marathoners or triathletes training twice a day can be at risk of not getting enough calcium in the diet to achieve a positive calcium balance.

Dr Michael Colgan, a renowned New Zealand research scientist believes athletes both male and female, and especially females with amenorrhoea need to supplement between 1000-2000mg of calcium per day.

Supplementation needs should always be assessed in relation to what is actually being obtained from the diet. Dietary intake should therefore always be assessed, along with identifying factors that could potentially increase calcium excretion e.g. high sodium and phosphorous diets, high protein diets, and an overall high "acidic" load. Knowledge should also be sought as to the types of calcium available and their rates of absorption.

Practical Suggestions to Increase Intake of Calcium and Iron

Eat low-fat dairy foods such as skimmed milk and natural yogurt daily

Add 100g of tofu and sunflower seeds to stir-frys and salads

Add almonds, dried figs and seeds to breakfast cereals

Add blanched spinach to scrambled or poached eggs

Use Tahini (sesame seed spread) on bread and crackers or add a tsp to natural yogurt

Eat plenty of dark green leafy vegetables such as kale, broccoli, watercress and spinach. Always steam or lightly cook brocolli, kale, cabbage and spinachto keep nutrients locked in.

Try soft-bony fish (tinned salmon, sardines, pilchards) as a topping on baked potatoes or wholegrain toast

Eat vitamin-C rich foods to enhance the absorption of iron (i.e. plenty of fresh fruit and colourful vegetables)

Be aware of substances that interfere with iron absorption (e.g. phytates found in bran, and tannin in tea).

Try NOT to drink tea and coffee with food

Many healthy, strong and fit vegans normally prove how healthy the vegan diet is daily. There is nothing humans need that cannot be obtained from a well balanced vegan diet. A vegan diet is suitable for humans of every age, as the American Dietetic Association and Dietitians of Canada acknowledge.

As shown, veganism can indeed be a way of life for female athletes. Iron and calcium intake can be obtained readily through non animal products. The following chapters are dedicated to providing inspiration on how varied vegan recipes can be.

Chapter 5: Vegan Recipes

There are a myriad of easy vegan recipes available nowadays to satisfy the tastes and needs of every vegan. Be it breakfasts, lunches, dinners, desserts, snacks or healthy treats, you can find an infinite number of recipes to try out.

With veganism becoming increasingly popular nowadays, many folk on the vegan diet are in desperate need for quick and easy vegan recipes to accommodate their busy lifestyle. Fortunately over the past couple of decades an abundance of vegan recipe ideas and information has emerged to cater for the needs of this ever-growing veganism lifestyle.

Below are some quick and easy vegan recipe ideas for your breakfast, lunch and dinners:

Vegan Breakfast Recipes and Ideas

Pancakes

Stir together in a bowl: 1 Cup flour, 1 Tbsp. sugar, 2 Tbsp. baking powder, and a pinch of salt. Add 1 Cup Soy/Rice/Coconut milk and 2 Tbsp. oil. Mix ingredients together until batter is smooth. In a hot, oiled frying pan, spoon in large spoonfuls of the mixture. Flip sides when bubbles start to appear (approximately 2 minutes per side). Add more oil to frying pan as needed. Serve pancakes with maple syrup, agave nectar, molasses, soy yogurt, fruit, berries, or another topping of your choice.

Fruit Smoothie

For those who have a blender, making a breakfast smoothie is a super easy and quick vegan breakfast option. Simply blend together your choice of a mixture of the following ingredients: soy/rice/coconut milk, soy/coconut yogurt, berries, bananas, dates, raisins, maple syrup, molasses, agave nectar, cacao powder, grated vegan chocolate, flaked/slithered almonds, crushed brazil nuts, flax seeds, LSA mix, oats, ice-cubes. Serve in a tall glass.

Vegan Lunch Recipes and Ideas

Tofu & Vegetable Stir-Fry

Cook tofu-nuggets in a hot oiled pan over high heat for 3 minutes or until golden and cooked through. Remove from pan. Next, stir fry (in peanut oil, for taste) some sliced carrots, baby-corns, snow-peas, broccoli or another vegetable of choice, on high heat for approximately 1 minute. Next add a few large Tbsps. (up to ¼ Cup) of vegetable stock liquid to pan, continue tossing vegetables, and cook for 3-4 minutes. Add tofu back to pan and continue to stir-fry for 1 minute more. Add salt and pepper, plus 1-2 tsp. sesame oil to taste. Eat alone or with rice or noodles.

Crackers with Many Toppings

For the very busy vegan, you can't get an easier lunch than crackers. But don't assume that just because you're eating crackers means lunch has to be boring. Firstly, find in your supermarket or health store some gourmet vegan crackers and crispbreads. Buy an assortment of them. Next, know your topping options. Suggestions are as follows:

Avocado, salt & pepper
Soy spread, tomato, salt, pepper
Tomato, vegan "cheese", salt, pepper
Peanut butter, almond spread
Tahini, maple syrup
Vegan hummus dip, beetroot dip, sun-dried tomato dip
Soy spread, salad
Soy spread, sun-dried tomatoes, olives

Vegan Dinners Recipes and Ideas

Pasta With "White Sauce"

Cook your pasta and vegetables as per usual. To make a tasty vegan "white sauce" heat 1 Tbsp. olive oil/soy spread in a frying pan, plus 1 heaped tsp. plain flour or cornflour. Stir on high heat for 1 minute. Next, add salt, pepper and dried herbs to taste. Next, you will be adding your soy/rice milk to the mixture - a little bit at a time, stirring constantly. Once desired consistency has been achieved, turn off heat and taste to serve. Adjust seasonings as necessary. Serve on top of pasta and vegetables. Top with grated vegan "cheese" if desired.

The Grandiose Garden Salad

If you are sick of salads, maybe you should start to gourmet them up a little more. Nobody can get tired of eating a proper, sustaining and mighty-flavorsome salad. To make the Grandiose Garden Salad, add the following ingredients together in a large bowl: 1 large packet of spinach and rocket leaves, chopped vine-ripened tomatoes or cherry tomatoes, a few spoonfuls of finely chopped sun-dried tomatoes, pitted olives, 1-2 chopped avocados, 1 finely sliced large cucumber, 1 cob of corn (either cooked or raw) - kernels removed and added to salad, ½ very thinly sliced red onion, tinned baby beetroot, and ½ cup of walnuts. To make the dressing, add together 2 Tbsp. olive oil, 1-2 tsp. lemon juice or balsamic vinegar, salt and pepper. Gently stir dressing into the salad. Enjoy the salad by itself, or with some toasted sourdough bread.

The above recipes are merely samples of some of the many thousands of ideas for quick and easy recipes for the vegan diet. Infact, nowadays one can create a dish that replicates their favorite foods, only without meat and dairy. With the convenience of countless vegan websites, blogs and vegan recipe e-books, one should have no trouble finding a recipe to 'clone' their favorite dish or sweet treat. Indeed, vegan food has never been boring!

Chapter 6: Bonus Recipes

Spinach Seasoned Korean Style

Ingredients:
1 lb. of spinach
2 tbsp. of soy sauce
1 tbsp. of sesame oil
1 tbsp. of sesame seeds
1 tbsp. of sesame salt*
2 cloves garlic (finely chopped)
2 tsp. of sugar

Instructions:
Gather the ingredients.
Blanch the spinach in boiling water for 30 seconds.
Remove the spinach quickly and rinse it in cold water. The easiest way to do this might be putting the spinach in a colander, turning on your kitchen faucet and then letting the water run over it.
Gently squeeze the vegetable to remove excess water. You can also try to shake the excess water from the spinach in the colander if you don't have the time or inclination to do so by hand.
Mix the soy sauce, sesame oil, seeds, salt, garlic, and sugar, and mix all of these ingredients into the spinach. Use more or fewer of these ingredients depending on your preference or the preference of those dinner guests to which you plan to serve the salad.

Serve and enjoy.

Miso Vegetable Soup

<u>Ingredients</u>:
2 cups plus 3 tablespoons water, divided
2 tablespoons white rice
2 cups frozen stir-fry vegetables
1 12-ounce package extra-firm silken tofu, cut into small cubes
2 tablespoons miso
2 scallions, thinly sliced
1 teaspoon rice vinegar, or to taste
½ to 1 tsp. sugar, to taste

<u>Instructions</u>:
Bring 2 cups water and rice to a boil in a large saucepan over high heat. Cover, reduce heat to a gentle simmer and cook until the rice is just tender, 12 to 15 minutes.

Add stir-fry vegetables to the pot, increase heat to high and bring to a boil. Cook until the vegetables are heated through, stirring occasionally, 2 to 3 minutes. Add tofu and cook until heated through about 2 minutes. Remove from the heat.

Combine miso and the remaining 3 tablespoons water in a small bowl and stir to dissolve. Add the miso mixture, scallions, vinegar and sugar to the soup and stir to combine.

Tomato and Basil Soup
Ingredients

- 1 medium sized onion
- 1 clove garlic
- 2 tablespoons olive oil
- 8 cherry tomatoes/3 vine tomatoes
- 14oz/400g can plum tomatoes
- 1 teaspoon dried basil or 5 leaves of fresh basil
- ¼ pint/150ml water
- 1 teaspoon salt
- pepper

Instructions

1. Chop onion and tomatoes. Finely slice garlic. Sauté in olive oil onion, tomatoes, garlic, and basil.
2. Add the canned tomatoes, salt and pepper. Cover the pan and let it simmer for 30 minutes on low heat.
3. Transfer to a blender or food processor and blend until smooth.

Cauliflower and Mushrooms Bake

Ingredients:
- 3 cups cauliflower flowerets
- 1 cup fresh mushroom, chopped
- ½ cup red onion, chopped
- 1/3 cup green onion, chopped
- 2 garlic cloves, finely chopped
- 2 teaspoons apple cider vinegar
- 2 teaspoons lemon juice
- ½ teaspoon salt
- ¼ teaspoon pepper
- 1 tablespoon olive oil

Instructions:
1. Preheat the oven to 350 degrees F. Lightly grease a baking pan.
2. Meantime, combine red onion, cauliflower, olive oil, garlic, mix mushroom, apple cider vinegar, lemon juice, salt and pepper in a bowl. Mix well.
3. Pour mixture into the greased baking pan.
4. Place inside the oven and bake for 45 minutes. Stir.
5. When vegetables are golden brown and tender, remove from the oven. Garnish with green onions. Serve.

Vegan Brownies with Walnuts

Ingredients:
- ½ cup semisweet chocolate chips, vegan
- 1/3 cup walnuts
- 1 dash cinnamon
- ½ tsp baking soda
- 1/3 cup cocoa powder
- ¾ cup unbleached white flour
- 1 tsp vanilla
- 1 cup applesauce, unsweetened
- ½ tsp salt
- 2 tsp baking powder
- ½ cup raw sugar

Instructions:
1. Preheat the oven to 350 degrees F. Grease baking pan with oil.
2. Meanwhile, in a bowl, put together vanilla, applesauce, and sugar.
3. Whisk the flour, baking soda, baking powder, cocoa and salt in a separate bowl. Add the cinnamon if using.
4. Create a well in the center of the dry ingredients. Scoop the applesauce mixture in the middle. Whisk until combined. Add in chocolate chips and walnuts. Stir.
5. Pour in a pan. Bake for 30 minutes. Let cool completely before slicing and serving.

Harvest Vegan Nut Roast

Ingredients

1/2 cup chopped celery 2 onions, chopped

3/4 cup walnuts

3/4 cup pecan or sunflower meal 2 1/2 cups soy milk

1 teaspoon dried basil

1 teaspoon dried oregano 3 cups bread crumbs

salt and pepper to taste

Directions

Preheat oven to 350 degrees F (175 degrees C). Lightly oil a loaf pan.

In a medium size frying pan, saute the chopped celery and the onion in 3 teaspoons water until cooked.

In a large mixing bowl combine the celery and onion with walnuts, pecan or sunflower meal, soy milk, basil, oregano, bread crumbs, salt and pepper to taste; mix well. Place mixture in the prepared loaf pan.

Bake for 60 to 90 minutes; until the loaf is cooked through.

Curry Rice

Ingredients

- 2 tablespoons olive oil
- 1 tablespoon minced garlic black pepper to taste
- 1 tablespoon ground cumin, or to taste
- 1 tablespoon ground curry powder, or to taste
- 1 tablespoon chili powder, or to taste
- 1 cube vegetable bouillon 1 cup water
- 1 tablespoon soy sauce
- 1 cup uncooked white rice

Directions

Heat olive oil in a medium saucepan over low heat. Sweat the garlic; when the garlic becomes aromatic, slowly stir in pepper, cumin, curry powder and chili powder. When spices begin to fry and become fragrant, stir in the bouillon cube and a little water.

Increase heat to high and add the rest of the water and the soy sauce. Just before the mixture comes to a boil, stir in rice. Bring to a rolling boil; reduce heat to low, cover, and simmer 15 to 20 minutes, or until all liquid is absorbed.

Remove from heat and let stand 5 minutes.

Fajitas

Ingredients

1/4 cup olive oil

1/4 cup red wine vinegar 1 teaspoon dried oregano 1 teaspoon chili powder garlic salt to taste

salt and pepper to taste 1 teaspoon white sugar

2 small zucchini, julienned

2 medium small yellow squash, julienned

1 large onion, sliced

1 green bell pepper, cut into thin strips

1 red bell pepper, cut into thin strips
2 tablespoons olive oil

1 (8.75 ounce) can whole kernel corn, drained

1 (15 ounce) can black beans, drained

Directions

In a large bowl combine olive oil, vinegar, oregano, chili powder, garlic salt, salt, pepper and sugar. To the marinade add the zucchini, yellow squash, onion, green pepper and red pepper.

Marinate vegetables in the refrigerator for at least 30 minutes, but not more than 24 hours.

Heat oil in a large skillet over medium-high heat. Drain the vegetables and saute until tender, about 10 to 15 minutes. Stir in the corn and beans; increase the heat to high for 5 minutes, to brown vegetables.

Veggie Salad

Ingredients:
½ pc cucumber, peeled and chopped thinly
2 pcs red tomatoes, chopped
5 pcs Romain lettuce leaves, torn into pieces
2 pcs regular-sized onions, minced
1 small-sized red bell pepper, chopped
1 pc carrots, chopped
½ small-sized clove garlic, minced
1 tbsp. lemon juice
a pinch of salt
1 tsp. water

Directions:
1. In a mixing bowl, mix all the ingredients using a spatula or a mixing spoon.
2. Do not add any salad dressings such as mayonnaise or balsamic vinegar. The lemon juice and salt are enough to add flavor to your salad.
3. Consume immediately.

"Garlic Spinach"
Ingredients:
- 1 ½ lb. baby spinach leaves
- 2 tsp kosher salt
- 2 tbsp. olive oil
- 2 tsp chopped garlic
- ¾ tsp ground black pepper
- 1 pc lemon

Directions:
1. Make sure to rinse the spinach under cold, running water. Then let it dry.
2. Using a large pot, sauté the garlic using olive oil for 1 minute. Make sure the garlic does not turn brown before adding the spinach. Add salt and pepper and lightly mix the ingredients. Cover the pot and cook for 2 minutes over medium heat. Make the spinach is not overcooked before serving. Squeeze some lemon juice and sprinkle a pinch of kosher salt on the finished product. Then serve immediately.

Rosemary Veggies - Roasted"

Ingredients:

½ pound turnips (cut into ½ -3/4-inch thick, ¼-inch length)

½ lb. carrots (cut into 1 ¼ - 1 1/2 –inch length, 1/4 –inch thick)

½ lb. parsnips (cut into 1 ¼ - 1 1/2 –inch length, 1/4 –inch thick)

½ lb. sweet potatoes (cut into ½ -3/4-inch thick, 1/4 –inch length)

2 medium-sized shallots, peeled

¼ tsp ground black pepper

2 tbsps. extra-virgin olive oil

6 cloves garlic (with skin)

¾ tsp kosher salt

2 tbsps. fresh rosemary needles

Directions:

1. Set the oven to 400°F.
2. Mix all the ingredients in a 9x13-inch baking dish. Roast the vegetables for 25 minutes until brown and tender. Toss and roast again for 20-25 minutes. Then serve hot.

Healthy Green Smoothie

Ingredients
1 cup fresh spinach
1/2 teaspoon mint extract or to taste
1/4 teaspoon peppermint liquid stevia (optional)

Directions:
1. Gather the ingredients.
2. Add them to a high powered blender
3. Turn on blender
4. Add them to glass and freeze for 5 minutes
5. Serve

Vegetable Lentil Soup

Ingredients
- 2 cups kale, chopped
- 1 ½ cups vegetable broth
- 1 ½ cups tomatoes, diced
- 1 ½ cups carrots, diced
- 1 ½ cups zucchini, diced
- 1 ½ cups yellow onions, diced
- 1 ¼ cups dried lentils, rinsed and picked over
- 1 cup of water
- 2 tbsp garlic, minced
- 2 tbsp olive oil
- 1 ½ tbsp dried basil
- 1 ½ tbsp thyme
- 1 tbsp fresh lemon juice
- Salt and ground black pepper to taste
- Parmesan cheese, for toppings

Instructions
1. Heat the oil in a pot over medium-high heat. Sauté the onions and garlic for 2 minutes. Then, add the carrots and sauté for 3 more minutes.

2. Pour the tomatoes and vegetable broth in the pot.

3. Add in the lentils, thyme, and basil. Season with pepper and salt to taste. Mix well.

4. Bring the mixture to a boil. Then, reduce the heat to medium-low. Cover the pot and simmer for 30 minutes. Stir the mixture occasionally to prevent burning.

5. Add the kale and zucchini. Simmer for 10 more minutes.

6. Mix in the lemon juice and at most 1 cup of water to thin the soup. Stir well.

7. Top with parmesan cheese and serve while warm.

Red Lentil Soup

Ingredients

1 tablespoon peanut oil 1 small onion, chopped
1 tablespoon minced fresh ginger root
1 clove garlic, chopped 1 pinch fenugreek seeds
1 cup dry red lentils
cup butternut squash - peeled, seeded, and cubed
1/3 cup finely chopped fresh cilantro
cups water
1/2 (14 ounce) can coconut milk 2 tablespoons tomato paste
1 teaspoon curry powder 1 pinch cayenne pepper 1 pinch ground nutmeg salt and pepper to taste

Directions

Heat the oil in a large pot over medium heat, and cook the onion, ginger, garlic, and fenugreek until onion is tender.

Mix the lentils, squash, and cilantro into the pot. Stir in the water, coconut milk, and tomato paste. Season with curry powder, cayenne pepper, nutmeg, salt, and pepper. Bring to a boil, reduce heat to low, and simmer 30 minutes, or until lentils and squash are tender.

Printed in Great Britain
by Amazon